SECOND EDITION

The Winky Cherry System
OF TEACHING YOUNG CHILDREN TO SEW

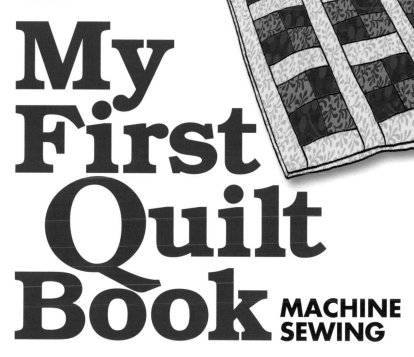

My First Quilt Book MACHINE SEWING

by Winky Cherry

edited by Linda Wisner, Jeannette Schilling, Pati Palmer, and Ann Gosch
designed by Linda Wisner

This book belongs to

_____

A Letter to Parents, Teachers, and Grown-ups

Quilting began as a plain and practical way to sew for warmth and protection. Today quilt making is an art form. Since the American Colonial innovation of mixing pieced blocks with plain blocks and stitching the patchwork pattern, quilt making—no longer a necessary part of housekeeping—has evolved into a creative, contemporary pastime.

I taught boys and girls sewing skills and, as a result, life skills, for over 20 years. In *My First Quilt Book*, the sixth level of **The Winky Cherry System of Teaching Young Children to Sew**,™ beginners are introduced to the concept of a quilt—three layers made up of a quilt top, batting and backing. A beginner then makes a pieced quilt with 10" One Patch blocks or the Four Patch blocks learned in *My First Patchwork Book*.

The quilt-making process is divided into four parts: **GETTING READY TO SEW, MAKING THE QUILT TOP, ADDING THE QUILT BACKING AND BATTING,** and **FINISHING THE QUILT** with ties and optional quilting stitches. Children learn to follow a quilt plan, use a template to make fabric squares, stitch straight lines following a seam guide, match cross seams, baste, tie, and use shapes to make designs for quilting stitches.

A child's first quilt is finished with the pillow-making process rather than binding. This first quilt is held together with ties so the quilt may be used while the child makes quilting stitches over a period of several weeks.

After the first quilt-making experience, a child will enjoy the math challenge of planning and making blocks and quilts in other sizes. Quilt plans are included for additional easy beginner quilt designs, including the very simple whole-cloth quilt and a strip quilt, which does not require matching cross seams.

Sewing classes may be built around each of the books in the "**My First...**" series. I have created teaching information, which is available from Palmer/Pletsch at www.palmerpletsch.com.

Winky Cherry
Winky Cherry

Second Edition copyright © 2011by Palmer/Pletsch Publishing
Original copyright © 1997. Third printing 2011.
Illustrations by Jeannette Schilling, Kate Pryka, and Linda Wisner

Library of Congress Catalog Card Number TBD
Published by Palmer/Pletsch Publishing,
1801 NW Upshur, Portland, OR 97209
www.palmerpletsch.com
Printed in the USA

ISBN 978-0-935278-90-3

2

Once upon a time someone made the first quilt and this is how!

The first QUILTS were filled with leaves, grass, feathers, or animal hair.
QUILTS have been used to
cover windows and doors,
and QUILTED CLOTHES are warm to wear.

QUILT BATTING
is sandwiched between
one piece of fabric
for the **QUILT TOP**
and one piece of fabric
for the **QUILT BACKING**.

QUILTING STITCHES or **TIES**
go through the three **LAYERS**
to hold them together like
toothpicks in a sandwich.

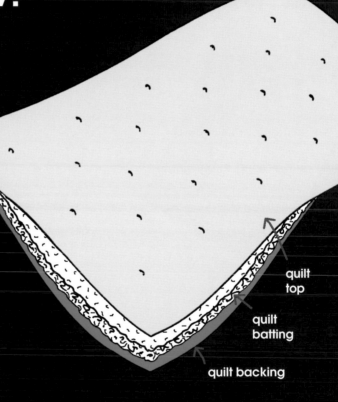

quilt
top

quilt
batting

quilt backing

Would *you* like to make a quilt now?

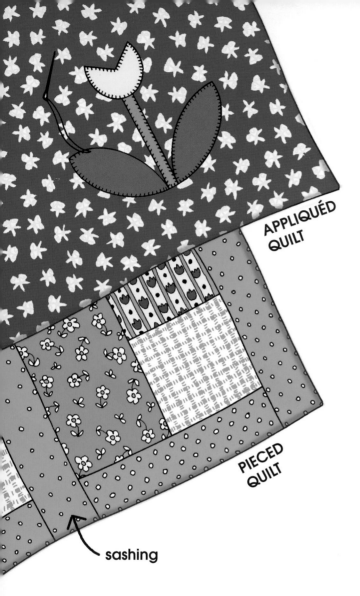

APPLIQUÉD QUILT

PIECED QUILT

sashing

ABOUT QUILTS

A QUILT TOP

can be made with pieces of fabric sewn together or it can be made from one piece of fabric like the WHOLE CLOTH QUILT on page 3. Appliqué may be added to any quilt top.

To APPLIQUÉ, stitch fabric shapes on top of a background.

To PIECE, stitch fabric pieces together with seams.

A BLOCK IS PART OF A PIECED QUILT TOP.

Most QUILT BLOCKS have a history and a name. A QUILT can have more than one BLOCK design or all the BLOCKS can be the same.

SASHING is a strip of fabric stitched between and around the blocks.

QUILTING STITCHES

are running stitches you can see on the QUILT TOP and QUILT BACKING that hold the quilt layers together with creative stitched designs.

A TIED QUILT

has pieces of yarn that go through all three layers of the quilt and are knotted to hold them in place.

A QUILT PLAN

shows the shape and size of the quilt, the shape of pieces in the QUILT TOP, and the supplies you will need.

The NAME of a QUILT tells about the design of the QUILT TOP.

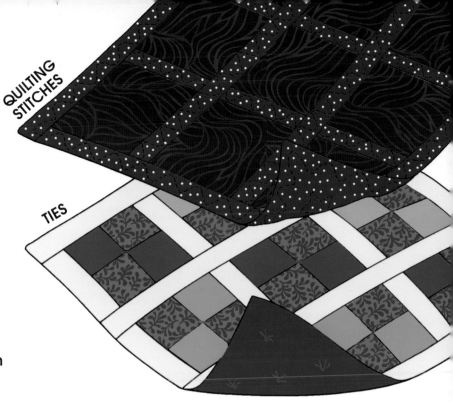

Someday you can design a new QUILT PLAN and name it. QUILT MAKING is a CREATIVE thing to do.

RULES FOR QUILT MAKING

1. **MAKE A SMALL QUILT BEFORE CHOOSING TO MAKE A LARGE PROJECT.**
   Setting limits makes it easier to finish what you start and learn something new.

2. **USE A QUILT PLAN.** The plan helps you organize and design your project.

3. **CHOOSE COLORS AND THE SIZE OF THE QUILT BEFORE SHOPPING FOR FABRIC.** Consider where you will use it when you choose it.

4. **Use 100% COTTON WOVEN FABRIC.** Other fabrics present challenges a beginner does not need.

5. **PREPARE THE FABRIC.** Preshrink and press fabric. Wrinkles don't look nice in the finished quilt. Remove any selvage (finished) edges and straighten all the edges. The fabric will be easier to cut and sew.

6. **USE A TEMPLATE.** An accurate piecing pattern is called a **TEMPLATE**. **PERFECT TEMPLATES** make piecing blocks together easy.

7. **MEASURE, CUT and STITCH ACCURATELY** using a **SEAM GUIDE**.
   The pieces fit together if the cut pieces are the same size as the template and seam allowances are all the same width. Straight stitching is important.

8. **MATCH EDGES AND CROSS SEAMS.** Take the time to line up seams, match and pin before sewing the pieces together.

9. **PRESS SEAMS TO ONE SIDE AFTER YOU SEW.**
   Press both sides of the seam allowance to one side, toward the darker fabric.

10. **FIX MISTAKES.** Learn from experience. When you understand how you did what you did, you will know how to undo a boo-boo and fix it.

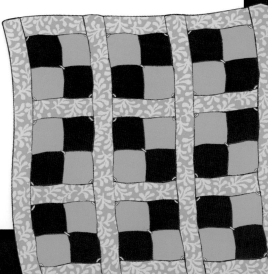

11. **USE A CHECKLIST.** A list helps you organize your work and remember what to do.

OPTIONAL:

embroidery hoop for hand quilting
T-square with 12" ruler for template making
template plastic or poster board for templates
quilting templates for quilting stitch designs

You may also ask your local quilt store's clerks
to recommend their favorite quilting tools.

- ❏ **straight quilter's pins**
- ❏ **special pins**
- ❏ **pincushion** with strawberry
  to sharpen the needle
- ❏ **needles**
  - Betweens sizes 3 to 5 for hand piecing and quilting
  - Embroidery sizes 3 to 5 for embroidery (see page 36).
  - Yarn needle for yarn ties (see pages 34-35).
- ❏ **thread** mercerized 100% cotton thread size 50
- ❏ **quilt plans**
- ❏ **template**
  - 5½" to make Four Patch blocks
  - or 10½" to make One Patch blocks
- ❏ **pencil**   ❏ **iron**
- ❏ **sandpaper #5**   ❏ **ironing board**
- ❏ **scissors** for cutting fabric
  AND another pair for cutting poster board
- ❏ **snippers** for cutting thread and yarn
- ❏ **tape measure**
- ❏ **sewing machine** for machine stitching
- ❏ **masking tape**
  to make a 1/4" seam guide on sewing machine
- ❏ **point turner**
- ❏ **washable yarn** for tying the quilt
- ❏ **quilt batting** at least 45" wide
  Ask your store for a stable batting for a tied quilt.
- ❏ **45" wide woven 100% cotton fabrics**
  More yardage is listed than necessary
  to allow for mistakes and so you can
  make a pillow out of leftovers to match the quilt.

**For fabric needed for the
42" x 42" NINE-BLOCK,
FOUR PATCH QUILT,
see the Quilt Plan Shopping List
on page 10.**

The FIRST PART OF QUILT MAKING is making a plan and getting the fabric ready to sew, before you learn how to stitch the quilt together. Plan your FIRST QUILT now.

8

CHOOSE A BLOCK FOR YOUR QUILT

Choose a FOUR PATCH BLOCK or a ONE PATCH BLOCK for the NINE-BLOCK QUILT this book teaches you to make.

10½" EMBROIDERY SAMPLERS from *My First Embroidery Book* can be ONE PATCH QUILT BLOCKS.

EACH BLOCK IN YOUR FIRST QUILT WILL BE A FINISHED 10" SQUARE.

Start with a 10½" or a 5½" unfinished SQUARE. Sew with a ¼" SEAM ALLOWANCE. (A seam allowance is the space between the stitching and the edge of the fabric.)

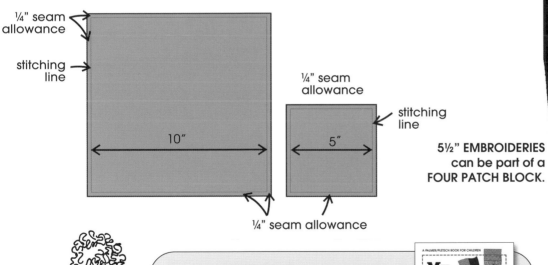

¼" seam allowance

stitching line

10"

¼" seam allowance

stitching line

5"

¼" seam allowance

5½" EMBROIDERIES can be part of a FOUR PATCH BLOCK.

If you made the FOUR PATCH BLOCK that *My First Patchwork Book* taught you, making FOUR PATCH BLOCKS for your first quilt will be easy to do.

USE A QUILT PLAN

A QUILT PLAN shows the size of the quilt, the block design, where colors go in the blocks, fabric designs, and the supplies you need.

A PLAN helps you GET READY TO SEW.

FRONT

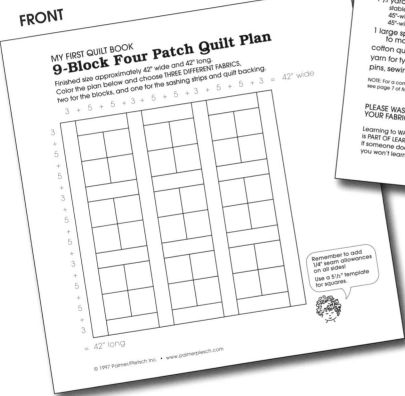

MY FIRST QUILT BOOK
9-Block Four Patch Quilt Plan

Finished size approximately 42" wide and 42" long.
Color the plan below and choose THREE DIFFERENT FABRICS,
two for the blocks, and one for the sashing strips and quilt backing.

3 + 5 + 5 + 3 + 5 + 5 + 3 + 5 + 5 + 3 = 42" wide

3
+
5
+
5
+
3
+
5
+
5
+
3
+
5
+
5
+
3
= 42" long

Remember to add 1/4" seam allowances on all sides!
Use a 5½" template for squares.

© 1997 Palmer/Pletsch Inc. • www.palmerplesch.com

BACK

MY FIRST QUILT BOOK
9-Block Four Patch Quilt Plan

The quilt shown here is an example of the types of fabrics you may choose.

SHOPPING LIST

1½ yards of fabric #1 for blocks
1½ yards of fabric #2 for blocks
3½ yards of fabric #3 for the sashing strips and quilt backing
1⅓ yards of quilt batting
 stable polyester batting for tied quilts OR
 45"-wide 100% cotton woven flannel OR
 45"-wide Pellon® fleece
1 large spool machine sewing thread to match background color of fabric
cotton quilting thread for optional hand quilting
yarn for tying the quilt
pins, sewing needles and yarn needle

NOTE: For a complete list of THINGS YOU WILL NEED see page 7 of My First Quilt Book.

PLEASE WASH, DRY AND IRON YOUR FABRIC BEFORE CLASS.

Learning to WASH and DRY fabric is PART OF LEARNING TO SEW. If someone does it for you, you won't learn what to do.

CHECKLIST FOR CHOOSING FABRICS

☐ WOVEN 100% COTTON fabric: 45" wide
☐ colored background— Choose one DARK, one LIGHT and one MEDIUM SHADE background.
☐ fabric design— Choose allover, different SCALE prints.

NOTE: For more information about choosing fabric, see page 12 of My First Quilt Book.

The **Winky Cherry System** OF TEACHING YOUNG CHILDREN TO SEW

SASHING STRIPS frame each **BLOCK** in this quilt design.

QUILT MATH is measuring the size of the FINISHED pieces and ADDING the SEAM ALLOWANCES.

ADD the numbers above to find out how big the QUILT will be.

The amount of fabric and BATTING to buy depends on the QUILT SIZE you choose.

COPY AND COLOR YOUR QUILT PLAN

COLOR two or three copies of your QUILT PLAN using your favorite colors. Choose which one to use when you look for fabrics for the blocks and sashing strips.

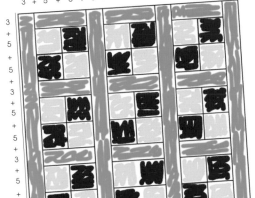

MY FIRST QUILT BOOK
9-Block Four Patch Quilt Plan

Finished size approximately 42" wide and 42" long.
Color the plan below and choose THREE DIFFERENT FABRICS,
two for the blocks, and one for the sashing strips and quilt backing.

3 + 5 + 5 + 3 + 5 + 5 + 3 + 5 + 5 + 3 = 42" wide

3 + 5 + 5 + 5 + 3 + 5 + 5 + 5 + 3 + 5 + 5 + 3

= 42" long

MY FIRST QUILT BOOK
9-Block Four Patch Quilt Plan

Finished size approximately 42" wide and 42" long.
Color the plan below and choose THREE DIFFERENT FABRICS,
two for the blocks, and one for the sashing strips and quilt backing.

3 + 5 + 5 + 3 + 5 + 5 + 3 + 5 + 5 + 3 = 42" wide

3 + 5 + 5 + 5 + 3 + 5 + 5 + 5 + 3 + 5 + 5 + 3

= 42" long

© 1997 Palmer/Pletsch Publishing

MY FIRST QUILT BOOK
9-Block Four Patch Quilt Plan

Finished size approximately 42" wide and 42" long.
Color the plan below and choose THREE DIFFERENT FABRICS,
two for the blocks, and one for the sashing strips and quilt backing.

3 + 5 + 5 + 3 + 5 + 5 + 3 + 5 + 5 + 3 = 42" wide

3 + 5 + 5 + 5 + 3 + 5 + 5 + 5

Remember
1/4" seam
on all sides
Use a 5½
for patch

Think about where you will use it when you choose it.

In your room? A gift for Grandma?

TAKE YOUR QUILT PLAN TO THE FABRIC STORE

**SHOP FOR SUPPLIES
WITH THE COLORED QUILT PLAN
TO FIND THE QUILT FABRIC.**

ASK QUESTIONS, **READ LABELS,**
and USE the CHECKLIST for the
supplies you choose.

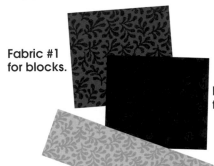

Fabric #1
for blocks.

Fabric #2
for blocks.

Fabric #3
for backing
and sashing strips.

CHECKLIST FOR CHOOSING THREE DIFFERENT FABRICS

☑ WOVEN 100% COTTON fabric 45" wide

☐ colored background—
Choose one DARK, one LIGHT, and one
MEDIUM **SHADE** background.

☐ fabric design—
Choose allover, different **SCALE** prints.

SHADE is
the lightness or darkness of a color.

SCALE is
the size of shapes in a design.

PREPARE THE FABRIC

WASH, DRY AND IRON.

Getting the fabric ready is part of making a QUILT.
If someone does it for you, you won't learn what to do!

> Ms. Wrinkle and Mr. Tuck mess up the fabric when it is not FLAT.
> You can use the IRON to fix that.

> *My First Patchwork Book* taught you to use an IRON. Do you remember what to do?

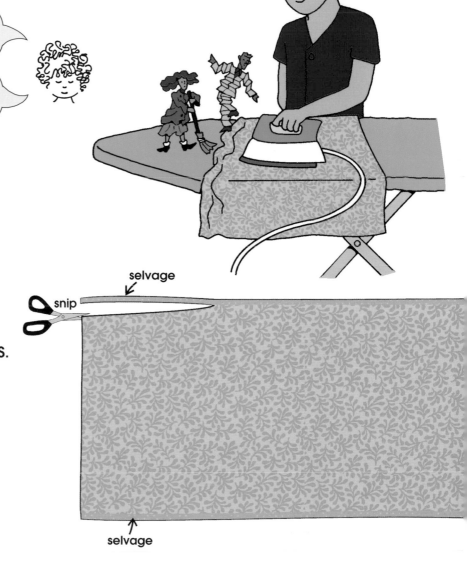

TEAR OFF THE SELVAGES.

New fabric has two cut edges and two SELF-EDGES called SELVAGES that are made in the weaving process.

Carefully snip then tear off the SELVAGES.

selvage

snip

selvage

13

MEASURE AND TEAR FABRIC #3

FOLD FABRIC #3 in HALF CROSSWISE. Make a SNIP on the FOLD, then TEAR at the snip to divide the large piece of fabric into TWO EQUAL PIECES.

Save one large piece of FABRIC #3 for the QUILT BACKING. Follow the directions on the next page to use the other half to cut sashing strips.

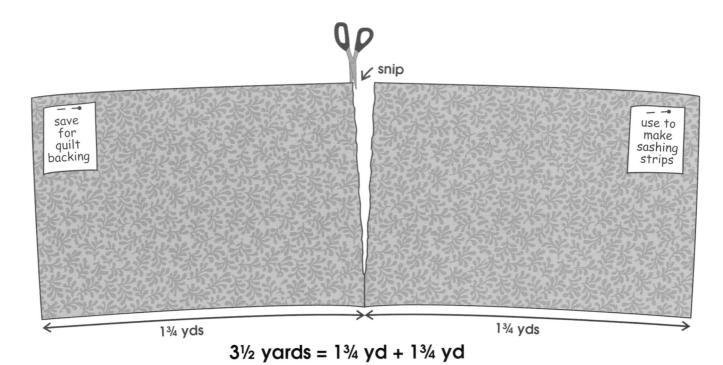

snip

save for quilt backing

use to make sashing strips

1¾ yds

1¾ yds

3½ yards = 1¾ yd + 1¾ yd

MAKE SEVEN LONG SASHING STRIPS FROM FABRIC #3

Measure seven 3½"-wide SASHING STRIPS.
Then snip and tear SASHING STRIPS.

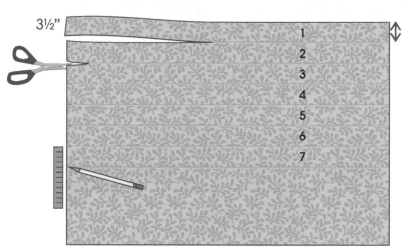

3½"

1
2
3
4
5
6
7

1¾ yard = 63 inches

MEASURE ACCURATELY BEFORE you CUT CAREFULLY.

Save BIG, leftover pieces.

MAKE 12 SHORT SASHING STRIPS

Using THREE of the LONG SASHING STRIPS, MEASURE and use
scissors to CUT each strip into four SHORT 10½" SASHING STRIPS.

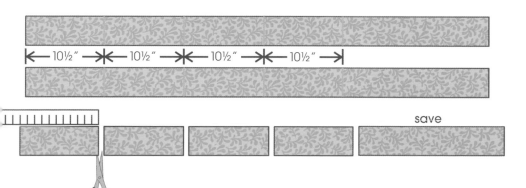

|←— 10½" —→|←— 10½" —→|←— 10½" —→|←— 10½" —→|

save

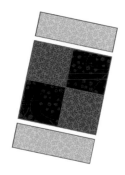

One SHORT STRIP
fits the side of a 10½"
stitched BLOCK.

GET READY STEP 9
PRESS AND SAVE THE SASHING STRIPS

Press the SASHING STRIPS FLAT.

HANG the PRESSED fabric SASHING STRIPS and the QUILT BACKING to use later.

Torn edges are curly. Did Ms. Wrinkle do that?

Use the leftover small pieces of fabric later to make a PILLOW that will match your QUILT.

for sashing strips

for Quilt back

Extra for pillow

USE A TEMPLATE TO DRAW THE FABRIC SQUARES

A TEMPLATE is a PATTERN made of poster board or plastic.
Machine quilt makers use a TEMPLATE that includes the
SEAM ALLOWANCE to draw a **CUTTING LINE** on the fabric.

> For a Four Patch Block quilt,
> use a 5½"-square template.
>
> For One Patch blocks,
> make a 10½" template.
> Turn to page 39
> to learn how.

> Before you draw, tape SANDPAPER
> to the table under the fabric, rough side up,
> to keep the fabric from moving.

DRAW AROUND THE TEMPLATE WITH A PENCIL.

Count the squares in your
QUILT PLAN. How many
squares do you need to draw?

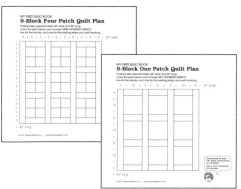

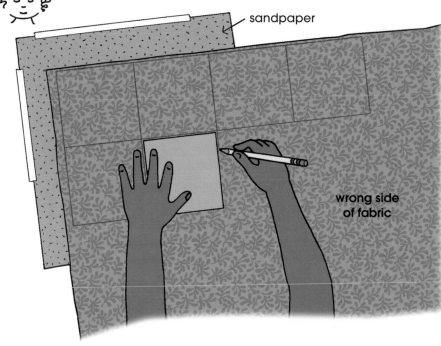

sandpaper

wrong side
of fabric

17

COUNT AND CUT THE FABRIC SQUARES

FOR A QUILT WITH 9 FOUR-PATCH BLOCKS, CUT 36 5½" FABRIC SQUARES.

CUT 18 SQUARES from FABRIC #1.

CUT 18 SQUARES from FABRIC #2.

FOR A QUILT WITH 9 ONE-PATCH BLOCKS, CUT NINE 10½" SQUARES.

If a CUT fabric square is NOT the same size as the TEMPLATE, draw and cut another square.

Make a few extra fabric square to use if you make a boo-boo.

ORGANIZE THE SQUARES

To make the ONE PATCH BLOCK QUILT

turn to page 20 to start QUILT MAKING'S SECOND PART.

To make the FOUR PATCH BLOCK QUILT

make nine piles of four fabric squares. In each pile, place
> two squares of FABRIC #1 and
> two squares of FABRIC #2.

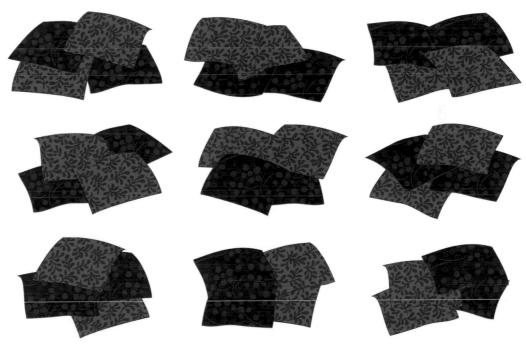

Making the QUILT TOP is the SECOND PART OF QUILT MAKING. Are you ready to start?

Make PATCHWORK BLOCKS. Make the QUILT TOP. Put the QUILT together.

MACHINE CHECKLIST
from *My First Machine Sewing Book*

> Choose the stitch size you are willing to rip if you make a boo-boo.

- [ ] 1. Pull the SPOOL and BOBBIN THREADS to be sure they each PULL FREELY.
- [ ] 2. Choose and set the size of the stitch.
- [ ] 3. Place the THREADS UNDER and BEHIND the PRESSER FOOT.
- [ ] 4. Place the fabric under the PRESSER FOOT.
- [ ] 5. Plant the needle AT THE BEGINNING OF THE STITCHING LINE.
- [ ] 6. Lower the PRESSER FOOT.
- [ ] 7. Back tack to LOCK the STITCHES at the beginning of the SEAM, using the REVERSE CONTROL.
- [ ] 8. Press the SPEED CONTROL to stitch to the end of the STITCHING LINE.
- [ ] 9. LOCK the STITCHES at the end of the SEAM.
- [ ] 10. Use the WHEEL to move the TAKE-UP LEVER to the highest position and to move the NEEDLE UP.
- [ ] 11. Lift the PRESSER FOOT.
- [ ] 12. Pull the fabric away from the machine.
- [ ] 13. Cut the THREADS leaving 6" of THREAD coming through the NEEDLE and 6" of THREAD coming from the BOBBIN.

STITCH AND PRESS THE NINE FOUR-PATCH BLOCKS NOW

> *My First Patchwork Book* taught you how to make a FOUR PATCH BLOCK.

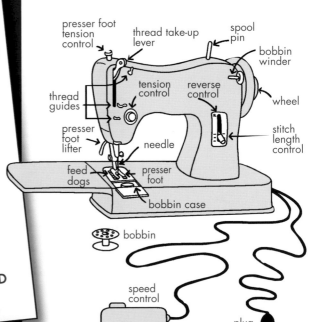

> Place TAPE on the machine 1/4" from the needle as a SEAM GUIDE, so the stitching will always be 1/4" from the cut edge.

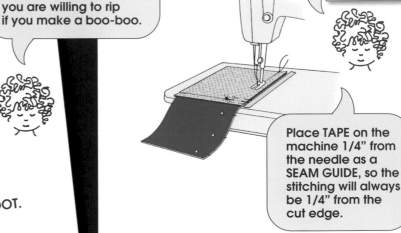

presser foot tension control · thread take-up lever · spool pin · bobbin winder · thread guides · tension control · reverse control · wheel · presser foot lifter · needle · stitch length control · feed dogs · presser foot · bobbin case · bobbin · speed control · plug

LAY OUT THREE ROWS TO SEW

Use four SHORT SASHING STRIPS and THREE BLOCKS for each row.

If you are making a One Patch Block, each row will look like this:

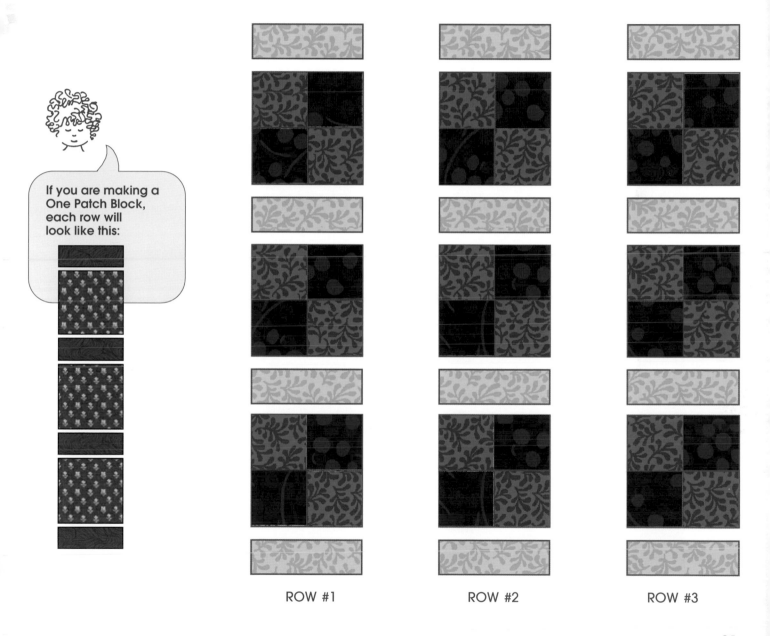

ROW #1   ROW #2   ROW #3

PIN EACH ROW

Place SASHING STRIPS RIGHT SIDES DOWN on top of BLOCKS.

FLIP over, match edges, and PIN SASHING STRIPS to the BLOCKS with pin points out and pin heads in.

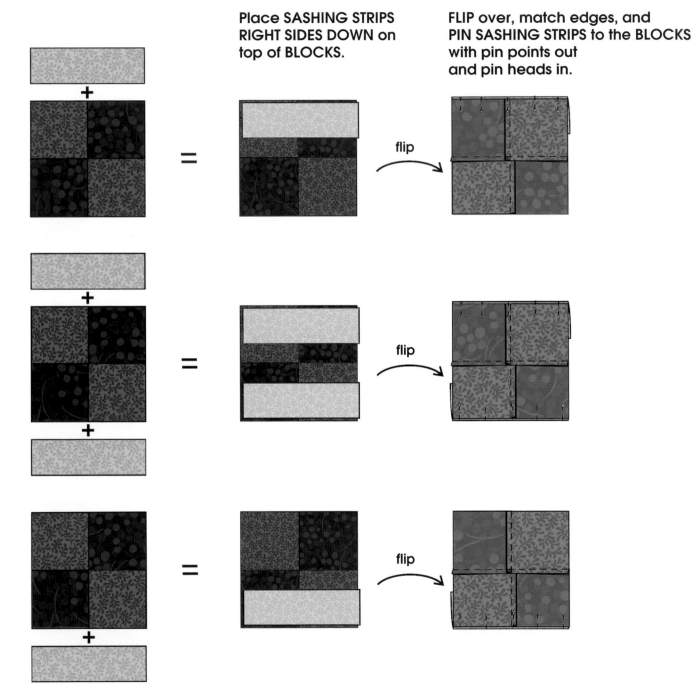

flip

flip

flip

STITCH AND PRESS EACH ROW

Use a 1/4" SEAM ALLOWANCE to stitch SASHING STRIPS to BLOCKS.

Start and stop stitching with a LOCK STITCH.

Guide the MATCHED EDGES along the edge of the SEAM GUIDE.

Now pin and stitch the pieces together to complete each row.

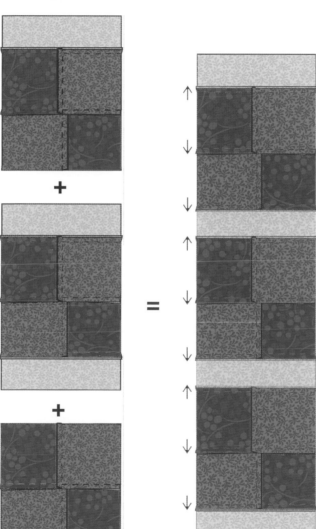

On the WRONG SIDE of the fabric, press the SEAM ALLOWANCES to SET THE STITCHES.

Press both sides of the SEAM ALLOWANCES toward the SASHING STRIPS as you press each row flat.

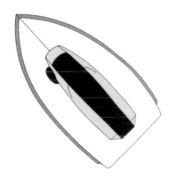

Make the machine go slow, and take the pins out as you sew.

CHECK THE ROWS

If the seams are all straight and the seam allowances are all the same size (1/4"), the cross seams will line up and the short sashing strips will make straight lines across the quilt. If these do not line up, rip and fix them now.

It is easier to fix boo-boos now, BEFORE you attach the long SASHING STRIPS.

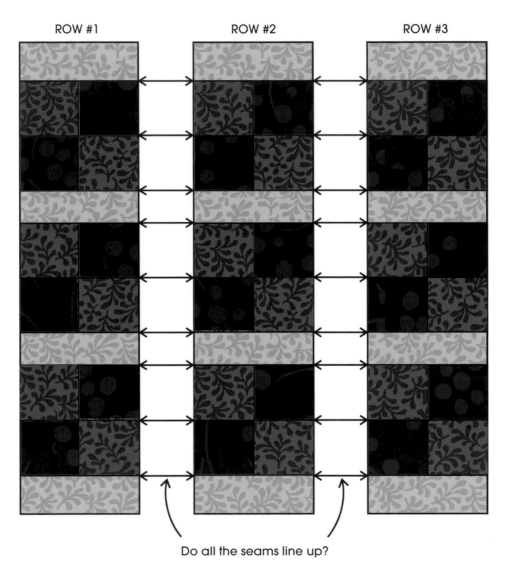

Do all the seams line up?

ATTACH A SASHING STRIP TO EACH SIDE OF ROW #2

LAY OUT, MATCH EDGES, PIN and STITCH
one LONG SASHING STRIP to each side of
ROW #2.

PRESS the long SEAM ALLOWANCES
toward the SASHING STRIPS.

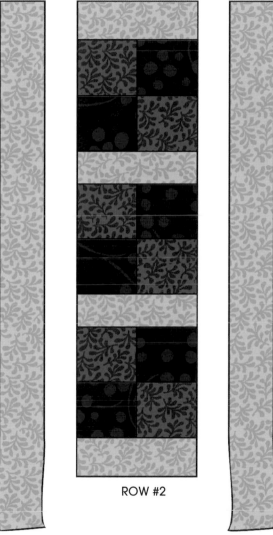

ROW #2

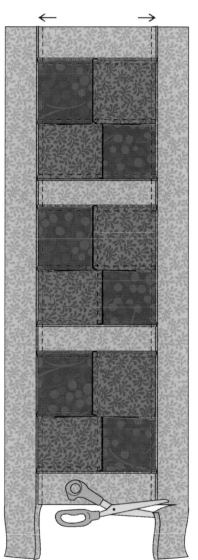

TRIM off
extra fabric
after you
sew.

Very long seams may be
heavy and awkward to sew.
Keep the fabric FLAT under the needle,
be careful, and go slow.

25

ATTACH A SASHING STRIP TO ONE SIDE OF ROW #1
AND ONE SIDE OF ROW #3

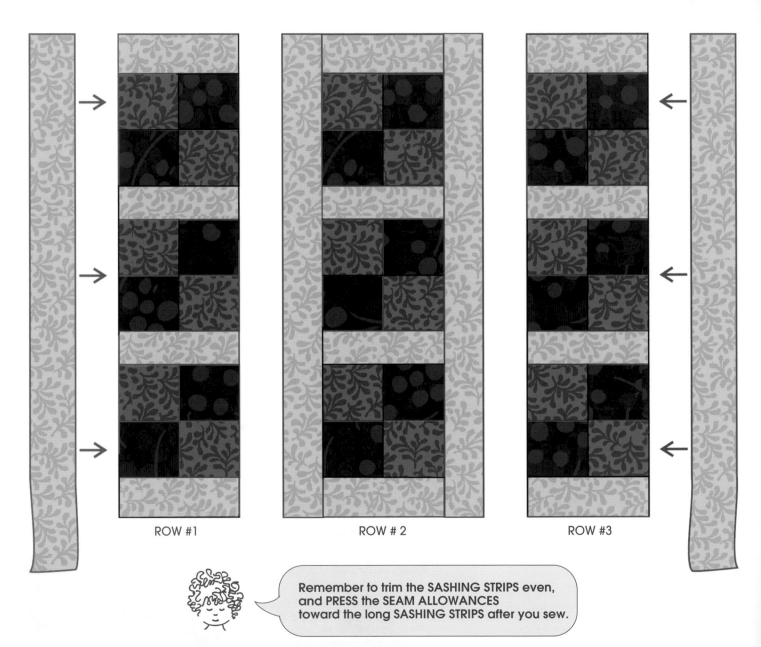

ROW #1

ROW # 2

ROW #3

Remember to trim the SASHING STRIPS even,
and PRESS the SEAM ALLOWANCES
toward the long SASHING STRIPS after you sew.

SEW THE THREE BIG ROWS TOGETHER WITH TWO LONG SEAMS

LAY OUT, MATCH EDGES, PIN and STITCH carefully. The SEAMS should make straight lines across the quilt.

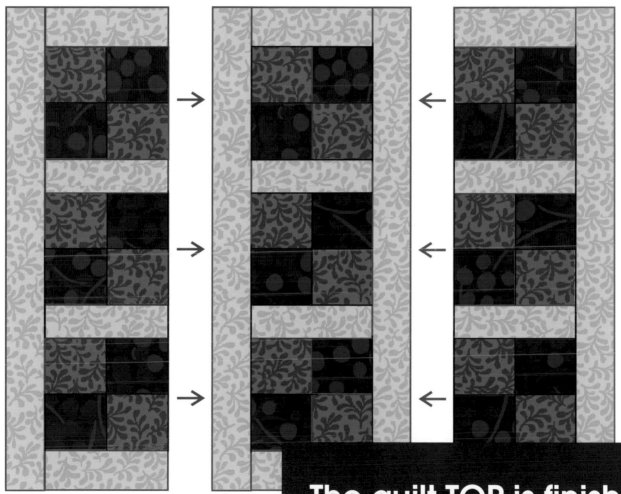

Remember to PRESS, put the pins away, and cut the long dangly threads. Check for any tucks or wrinkles.

The quilt TOP is finished. Accomplishment is fun! What a GREAT JOB you have done!

ADDING THE BATTING and the **QUILT BACKING** is the **THIRD PART** of QUILT MAKING. Find a BIG, FLAT WORK SPACE to LAY OUT, PIN, BASTE and STITCH the THREE BIG QUILT PIECES in place.

If you don't have a large table, WORK ON THE FLOOR.

Save the leftover fabric to make a pillow to match your QUILT.

MAKE A DIFFERENT KIND OF SANDWICH

Put the QUILT BACKING (fabric #3) and the QUILT TOP RIGHT SIDES TOGETHER on top of the QUILT BATTING. Smooth out the layers so there are no wrinkles.

Place a PIN diagonally in each corner to hold the three layers together.

Cut the QUILT BACKING and QUILT BATTING the same size as the QUILT TOP.

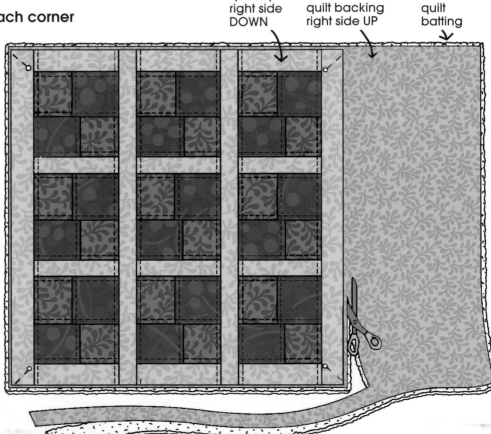

quilt top right side DOWN

quilt backing right side UP

quilt batting

MATCH, PIN, AND BASTE THE EDGES OF THE QUILT

BASTING STITCHES are TEMPORARY 1/2"-long running stitches that hold the QUILT layers together with the EDGES MATCHED until the machine stitching is finished. Keep basting stitches close to the edge so they will not get caught in the stitching when you machine-sew the 1/4" seam allowance.

Choose a BASTING thread color that's easy to see when you later remove the stitches used temporarily.

Don't lock the basting stitches!

Use pins to hold the three edges together while you BASTE.

Take out all the pins after you BASTE, and before you sew.

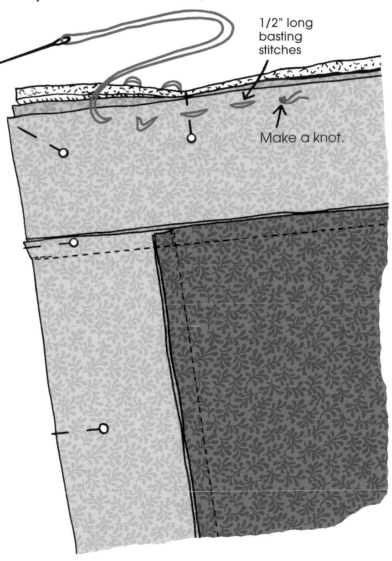

1/2" long basting stitches

Make a knot.

MACHINE STITCH AROUND THE EDGE OF THE QUILT

PLACE TWO SPECIAL PINS TO MARK AN OPENING.

Leave open
for turning.

Decide which two pins
will be your SPECIAL PINS.
They will remind you to
do something new.

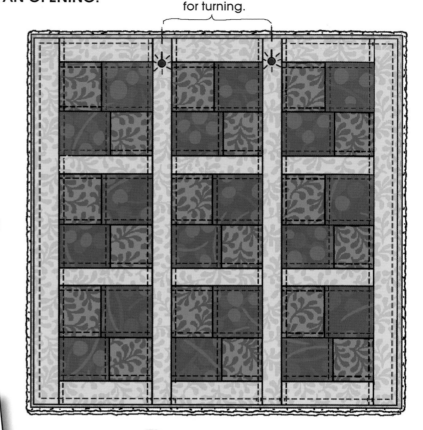

Leave an OPEN PLACE to turn the QUILT
RIGHT SIDE OUT after the machine stitching is finished.

Stitch a 1/4" SEAM ALLOWANCE following
the SEAM GUIDE TAPE. Lock the stitches
when you start and stop at the SPECIAL
PINS.

TURNING CORNERS CHECKLIST

- [x] Lift presser foot when needle is down in the corner.

- [x] Pivot (turn) the QUILT.

- [x] Match the fabric edge to SEAM GUIDE TAPE, lower PRESSER FOOT, and sew.

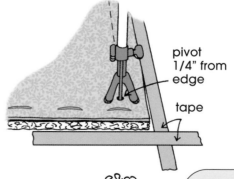

pivot
1/4" from
edge

tape

Add another piece of tape
1/4" in front of the needle
as a measuring guide
to turn corners.

TAKE OUT THE BASTING STITCHES

Pull the knots, or cut the thread and pull, to take out the BASTING THREAD when you know there are no tucks to fix after you sew.

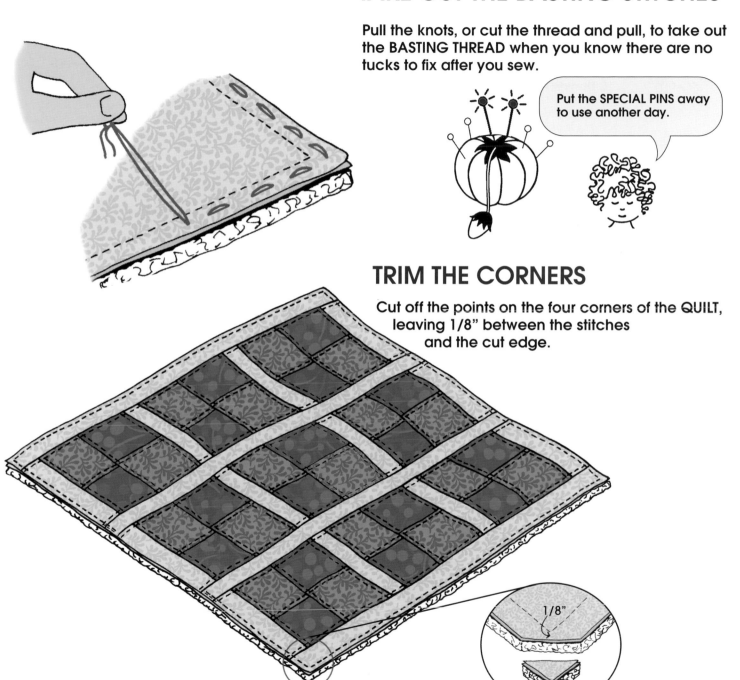

Put the SPECIAL PINS away to use another day.

TRIM THE CORNERS

Cut off the points on the four corners of the QUILT, leaving 1/8" between the stitches and the cut edge.

1/8"

TURN THE QUILT RIGHT SIDE OUT

A QUILT is BORN as you pull the RIGHT SIDE through. Celebrate the creation of something new!

Reach into the opening between the QUILT TOP and the QUILT BACKING, and PULL the QUILT out through the opening.

Use your pointer finger or a POINT TURNER to **FIND and POKE OUT ALL FOUR CORNERS.**

Use point turner inside the quilt.

HAND STITCH TO CLOSE THE OPENING

Fold in the 1/4" SEAM ALLOWANCE along the opening edges.

MATCH FOLDED EDGES and HOLD the folds together with pins.

OVERSTITCH the pinned edges together with needle and thread just as *My First Sewing Book* taught you. Remember to LOCK STITCH too.

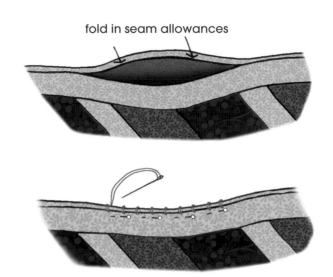

fold in seam allowances

BASTE AROUND THE EDGE OF THE QUILT, AND BASTE AN (optional) "X" FROM CORNER TO CORNER

Use 1"-long BASTING STITCHES to TEMPORARILY hold the QUILT TOP, QUILT BATTING, and QUILT BACKING flat in place while you tie the quilt or make QUILTING STITCHES to hold the layers together.

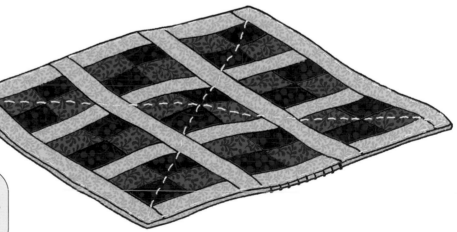

Remove the BASTING STITCHES AFTER the YARN TIES or QUILTING STITCHES are there to stay.

THE FOURTH and LAST PART of QUILT MAKING
is adding ties or stitches
to hold all the layers together,
as toothpicks in a sandwich do.

Traditionally, quilters use ties OR quilting stitches.
For this quilt, TIE the layers together FIRST and
LATER add designs with QUILTING STITCHES.

GET READY TO MAKE TIES

Measure yarn three times as long
as your arms reach wide,
as *My First Doll Book*
taught you.

Put the YARN through
the YARN NEEDLE's eye.

Match two cut ends
but DON'T make a knot.
You know what to do.

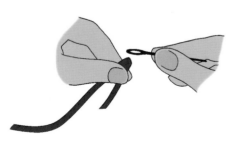

STITCH TIES THROUGH THE FOUR CORNERS AND IN THE CENTER OF EACH 10" BLOCK

MAKE TIES WITH THE KNOTS ON THE BACK OF THE QUILT.

TOP of quilt

Corners of quilt BLOCK

← Leave yarn tail on back LONG ENOUGH TO TIE.

Knots on the BACK will not get in the way when QUILTING STITCHES are added LATER (see page 37). Knots may be tied on TOP as decoration.

1. Poke the needle UP through the QUILT BACKING.

2. Pull the YARN all the way through the QUILT, leaving a SHORT TAIL on the QUILT back long enough to tie.

3. Poke the needle DOWN through the QUILT TOP and pull the YARN all the way through the QUILT.

4. Cut the LONG YARN to match the SHORT TAIL.

TIE AND TRIM THE YARN

Hold two pieces of yarn with each hand, and TIE a DOUBLE KNOT.

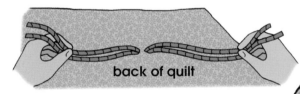

back of quilt

SNIP the YARN ENDS to 1".

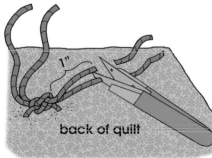

1"

back of quilt

Remove the basting stitches after all the knots are tied.

Now stitch your NAME, AGE, the DATE and the PLACE your QUILT was made! This makes the QUILT "talk" to you, and others in the future too!

A hundred years from now no one will know who made your QUILT unless you stitch a message in the QUILTS you sew.

Use a pencil to DRAW the letters and numbers on one quilt square.

Get a needle and embroidery thread ready to SEW.

"WOW! This is the FIRST QUILT my Great Grandma made in 1997 when she was 9 years old."

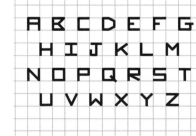

Start and stop needle here.

Stitches go through only the TOP layer of fabric, using a SCOOP STITCH.

My First Embroidery Book taught you HORIZONTAL, VERTICAL AND DIAGONAL stitches in squares under your name.

Those stitches and the LINES in this easy ALPHABET ARE THE SAME.

```
A B C D E F G
 H I J K L M
N O P Q R S T
 U V W X Y Z

1 2 3 4 5 6 7 8 9 0
```

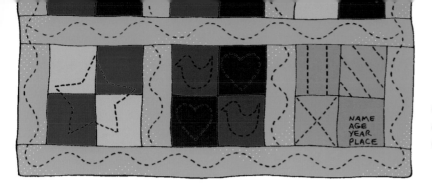

ADD QUILTING STITCHES

QUILTING STITCHES hold the quilt together and add to the QUILT DESIGN. Make QUILTING STITCHES on one block at a time.

> Putting a quilt together is called QUILT MAKING. Adding QUILTING STITCHES to attach the layers is called QUILTING.

CHOOSE A SHAPE AND MAKE A QUILTING TEMPLATE.

Find a QUILTING DESIGN TEMPLATE in a store, OR make plastic or poster board templates using new shapes you choose or paper pattern shapes from *My First Sewing Book.*

(The patterns are available at www.palmerpletsch.com.)

TRACE A SHAPE.

Use a pencil to TRACE around a SMALL shape in one square, or a BIG shape in a BLOCK, or draw a straight or wavy LINE DESIGN.

HAND STITCH.

Place the quilt in an embroidery hoop to keep the layers flat and stretched tight for smooth stitching. Use a running stitch on the pencil lines to make hand quilting stitches through the three quilt layers.

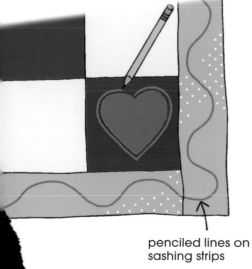

> Try to make your quilting stitches ALL THE SAME SIZE. Choose a length 1/8" to 1/4" long.
>
> (Experienced quilters use smaller needles and smaller stitches.)

penciled lines on sashing strips

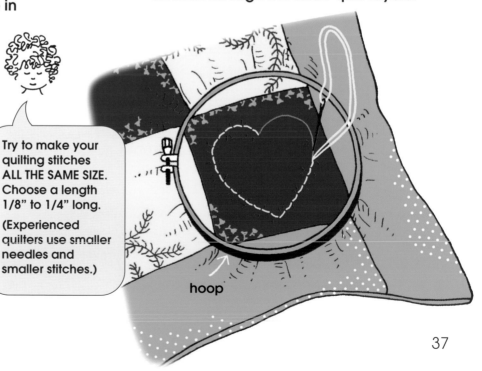
hoop

FRAME A BLOCK WITH STRIPS TO MAKE A PILLOW or DOLL QUILT

1. Make an extra FOUR PATCH quilt block.

2. Measure, cut, pin, and stitch SHORT SASHING STRIPS of leftover fabric #3 to the top and bottom of the BLOCK first.

3. Then measure, cut, pin, and stitch LONGER SASHING STRIPS to the sides of the BLOCK.

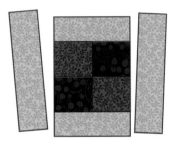

4. Cut a backing the same size as the FRAMED SQUARE, and for a doll quilt cut BATTING too.

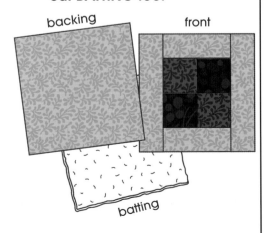

backing
front
batting

5. Pin, then sew, around the outside edges. Leave an opening for turning and stuffing.

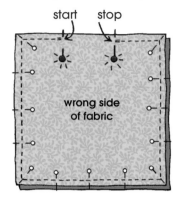

start   stop

wrong side of fabric

NOTE: If you are making a doll quilt, pin and stitch THREE layers together.

6. Trim the corner points (see page 31).

7. Turn the pillow or quilt RIGHT SIDE OUT through the opening. POKE the corners out with a POINT TURNER.

8. IF YOU ARE MAKING A PILLOW, fill it with stuffing now.

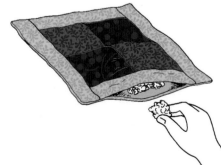

9. Overstitch the opening closed.

10. IF YOU ARE MAKING A DOLL QUILT, finish the framed block like a little quilt with ties. See page 35.

MAKE TEMPLATES FOR PIECING

TO MAKE YOUR OWN PLASTIC OR POSTER BOARD TEMPLATE:

1. Use a T-square to measure from one side of a SQUARE CORNER of the template material. Make a pencil mark.

2. Use the T-square to measure the same distance from the OTHER SIDE of the SAME SQUARE CORNER and make a SECOND pencil mark.

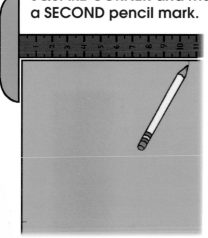

3. Move the T-square to draw a straight line from the FIRST pencil mark at least as long as the template will be.

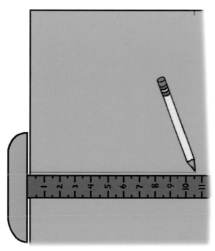

4. Move the T-square to draw a straight line from the SECOND pencil mark to make a square.

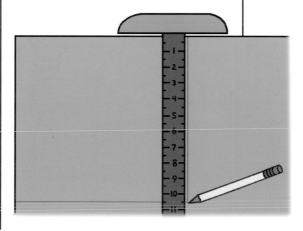

5. Cut out the TEMPLATE carefully to make a perfect square.

Learning GEOMETRY will help you make TEMPLATES for any shape you want to sew. MATH is important for QUILT MAKERS to know.

QUILT PLANS TO COPY AND COLOR

Use the loose quilt plans that come in the kit, complete with a shopping list and yardage information.

If you do not have separate quilt plans, enlarge the plans on this page, visit www.palmerpletsch.com, or call 1-800-728-3784 to order another set.

FRONT

MY FIRST QUILT BOOK
9-Block Four Patch Quilt Plan
Finished size approximately 42" wide and 42" long.
Color the plan below and choose THREE DIFFERENT FABRICS, two for the blocks, and one for the sashing strips and quilt backing.

3 + 5 + 5 + 3 + 5 + 5 + 3 = 42" wide

= 42" long

Remember to add 1/4" seam allowances on all sides! Use a 5 1/2" template for squares.

© 1997 Palmer/Pletsch Inc. • www.palmerpletsch.com

BACK

MY FIRST QUILT BOOK
9-Block Four Patch Quilt Plan
The quilt shown here is an example of the fabrics & colors you may choose.

SHOPPING LIST
1 1/2 yards of fabric #1 for blocks
1 1/2 yards of fabric #2 for blocks
3 1/2 yards of fabric #3 for the sashing strips and quilt backing
1 1/2 yards of quilt batting
stable polyester batting for tied quilts OR 45"-wide 100% cotton woven flannel OR 45"-wide Pellon® fleece
1 large spool machine sewing thread to match background color of fabric
cotton quilting thread for optional hand quilting
yarn for tying the quilt
pins, sewing needles and yarn needle

NOTE: For a complete list of THINGS YOU WILL NEED see page 7 of My First Quilt Book.

PLEASE WASH, DRY AND IRON YOUR FABRIC BEFORE CLASS.

Learning to WASH and DRY fabric is PART OF LEARNING TO SEW. If someone does it for you, you won't learn what to do.

CHECKLIST FOR CHOOSING FABRICS
☐ WOVEN 100% COTTON fabric: 45" wide
☐ colored background— Choose one DARK, one LIGHT and one MEDIUM SHADE background.
☐ fabric design— Choose allover, different SCALE prints.

40

MY FIRST QUILT BOOK
9-Block One Patch Quilt Plan
Finished size approximately 42" wide and 42" long.
Color the plan below and choose TWO DIFFERENT FABRICS, two for the blocks, and one for the sashing strips and quilt backing.

3 + 10 + 3 + 10 + 3 + 10 + 3 = 42" wide

= 42" long

Remember to add 1/4" seam allowances on all sides! Use a 10 1/2" template for squares.

© 1997 Palmer/Pletsch Inc. • www.palmerpletsch.com

MY FIRST QUILT BOOK
9-Block One Patch Quilt Plan
The quilt shown here is an example of the types of fabrics you may choose.

SHOPPING LIST
1 1/2 yards of fabric #1 for blocks
3 1/2 yards of fabric #2 for the sashing strips and quilt backing
1 1/2 yards of quilt batting
stable polyester batting for tied quilts OR 45"-wide 100% cotton woven flannel OR 45"-wide Pellon® fleece
1 large spool machine sewing thread to match background color of fabric
cotton quilting thread for optional hand quilting
yarn for tying the quilt
yarn needle
pins and needles

NOTE: For a complete list of THINGS YOU WILL NEED see page 7 of My First Quilt Book.

PLEASE WASH, DRY AND IRON YOUR FABRIC BEFORE CLASS.

Learning to WASH and DRY fabric is PART OF LEARNING TO SEW. If someone does it for you, you won't learn what to do.

CHECKLIST FOR CHOOSING FABRICS
☐ WOVEN 100% COTTON fabric 45" wide
☐ colored background— Choose one DARK, one LIGHT SHADE background.
☐ fabric design— Choose allover, different SCALE prints.

NOTE: For more information about choosing fabric, see page 12 of My First Quilt Book.

The Winky Cherry System OF TEACHING CHILDREN TO SEW

MY FIRST QUILT BOOK
12-Block Four Patch Quilt Plan
Finished size approximately 42" wide and 55" long.
Color the plan below and choose at least THREE DIFFERENT FABRICS.

3 + 5 + 5 + 3 + 5 + 5 + 3 + 5 + 5 + 3 = 42" wide

= 55" long

Remember to add 1/4" seam allowances on all sides! Use a 5 1/2" template for squares.

© 1997 Palmer/Pletsch Inc. www.palmerpletsch.com

MY FIRST QUILT BOOK
12-Block Four Patch Quilt Plan
The quilt shown here is an example of the types of fabrics you may choose.

SHOPPING LIST
1 1/2 yards of fabric #1 for blocks
1 1/2 yards of fabric #2 for blocks
3 1/2 yards of fabric #3 for the sashing strips and quilt backing
1 1/2 yards of quilt batting
stable polyester batting for tied quilts OR 45"-wide 100% cotton woven flannel OR 45"-wide Pellon® fleece
1 large spool machine sewing thread to match background color of fabric
cotton quilting thread for optional hand quilting
yarn for tying the quilt
pins, sewing needles and yarn needle

NOTE: For a complete list of THINGS YOU WILL NEED see page 7 of My First Quilt Book.

PLEASE WASH, DRY AND IRON YOUR FABRIC BEFORE CLASS.

Learning to WASH and DRY fabric is PART OF LEARNING TO SEW. If someone does it for you, you won't learn what to do.

CHECKLIST FOR CHOOSING FABRICS
☐ WOVEN 100% COTTON fabric: 45" wide
☐ colored background— Choose one DARK, one LIGHT and one MEDIUM SHADE background.
☐ fabric design— Choose allover, different SCALE prints.

NOTE: For more information about choosing fabric, see page 12 of My First Quilt Book.

The Winky Cherry System OF TEACHING CHILDREN TO SEW

MY FIRST QUILT BOOK
Strip Quilt Plan
Finished size approximately 42" wide and 42" long.
Color the plan below and choose THREE DIFFERENT FABRICS, two for the wide strips, and one for the narrow strips and quilt backing.

3 + 5 + 3 + 5 + 3 + 5 + 3 + 5 + 3 = 42" wide

42" long

Remember to add 1/4" seam allowances and 3 1/2" and 5 1/2" wide.

© 1997 Palmer/Pletsch Inc. • palmerpletsch.com

MY FIRST QUILT BOOK
Strip Quilt Plan
The quilt shown here is an example of the types of fabrics you may choose.

SHOPPING LIST
1 1/2 yards of fabric #1 for wide strips
1 1/2 yards of fabric #2 for wide strips
3 1/2 yards of fabric #3 for narrow strips and quilt backing
1 1/2 yards of quilt batting
stable polyester batting for tied quilts OR 45"-wide 100% cotton woven flannel OR 45"-wide Pellon® fleece
1 large spool machine sewing thread to match background color of fabric
cotton quilting thread for optional hand quilting
yarn for tying the quilt
pins, sewing needles and yarn needle

NOTE: For a complete list of THINGS YOU WILL NEED see page 7 of My First Quilt Book.

PLEASE WASH, DRY AND IRON YOUR FABRIC BEFORE CLASS.

Learning to WASH and DRY fabric is PART OF LEARNING TO SEW. If someone does it for you, you won't learn what to do.

CHECKLIST FOR CHOOSING FABRICS
☐ WOVEN 100% COTTON fabric 45" wide
☐ colored background— Choose one DARK, one LIGHT and one MEDIUM SHADE background.
☐ fabric design— Choose allover, different SCALE prints.

NOTE: For more information about choosing fabric, see page 12 of My First Quilt Book.

The Winky Cherry System OF TEACHING CHILDREN TO SEW

MY FIRST QUILT BOOK
Whole Cloth Doll Quilt Plan
Finished size approximately 13" wide and 20" long (doll size).
Color the plan below and choose TWO DIFFERENT FABRICS, one for the quilt top and one for the quilt backing.

15" wide

20" long

Cut the rectangles 13 1/2" x 20 1/2" and use a 1/4" seam allowance.

You can make a whole cloth quilt ANY size or shape you want it to be if you do the math and plan creatively.

© 1997 Palmer/Pletsch Inc. • palmerpletsch.com

MY FIRST QUILT BOOK
Whole Cloth Doll Quilt Plan
The quilt shown here is an example of the types of fabrics you may choose.

SHOPPING LIST
1 yard of fabric #1 for quilt top
1/2 yard of fabric #2 for quilt backing
1/2 yard of quilt batting
stable polyester batting for tied quilts OR 45"-wide 100% cotton woven flannel OR 45"-wide Pellon® fleece
1 small spool machine sewing thread to match background color of fabric
cotton quilting thread for optional hand quilting
yarn needle
pins and needles

NOTE: For a complete list of THINGS YOU WILL NEED see page 7 of My First Quilt Book.

PLEASE WASH, DRY AND IRON YOUR FABRIC BEFORE CLASS.

Learning to WASH and DRY fabric is PART OF LEARNING TO SEW. If someone does it for you, you won't learn what to do.

CHECKLIST FOR CHOOSING FABRICS
☐ WOVEN 100% COTTON fabric: 45" wide
☐ colored background— Choose one DARK and one LIGHT SHADE background.
☐ fabric design— Choose allover, different SCALE prints.

NOTE: For more information about choosing fabric, see page 12 of My First Quilt Book.

The Winky Cherry System OF TEACHING CHILDREN TO SEW